BURNOUT

A Spiritual Crisis on the Way Home

Stephen G Wright

For Loretta,

with every blessing,

Stephen Wright

Edinburgh . March 2011

This work is in part based on an original idea for nurses published in Nursing
Standard in 2006. I am grateful to RCN Publications for their kind permission
to use some of that material and develop it further for a general readership.

British Library Cataloguing in Publication Data
A catalogue record for this book is available from the British Library.

ISBN 978-0-9560303-4-4

Typeset and Printed on recycled paper by
Reeds Printers Limited
Southend Road, Penrith, Cumbria CA11 8JH
Tel: 01768 864214.

Contents

"Between the probable and the proved there yawns
A Gap. Afraid to jump, we stand absurd,
Then see behind us sink the ground and, worse
Our very standpoint crumbling. Desperate dawns
Our only hope: to leap into the Word
That opens up the shuttered universe."
H R Morris

1. Introduction

In the book "Coming Home" I describe many of the challenges we may encounter in spiritual exploration . Burnout is one of these, but it may occur amongst people who are not intentionally spiritually seeking and amongst those who may not be accustomed to seeing themselves as "spiritual". Nevertheless burnout, as this book explores, can be defined as a spiritual crisis full of suffering , but also full of potential for healing and transformation.

Burnout and stress are often described together and interchangeably in the literature, the one (burnout) being presumed to flow from an extreme experience of the other. There is no doubt that stress is closely associated with burnout, but this book offers a different perspective, based on the successful work of the Sacred Space Foundation, a charity based in the North of England set up to help those suffering from the extremes of stress and burnout. Stress is often the focus of the attention, and many studies highlight exceptionally high levels amongst the caring professions of all sorts – nurses, doctors, therapists, fire and police officers, teachers, social workers, clergy, aid workers and so on. It also affects lay people involved in caring situations such as those supporting a disabled person at home.

The bibliography at the end of this paper provides supporting references as well as illustrating its worldwide and cross-professional extent. An internet search for the word burnout, at the time of writing, revealed over 40 million hits!

The evidence for stress in the workplace is strong and produces high costs to organisations, currently running in excess of £4billion to the UK economy according to a Confederation of British Industry report. Gooding, in another report, suggests that each NHS Trust is losing on average £450,000 a year in stress related absence. Other high profile media accounts have indicated successful prosecutions of organisations which fail to reduce stress on their staff. Under UK law, an employer has a duty of care to employees to prevent harm from stress. When organisations fail to do this, employees can be successful in claiming substantial compensation through the courts.

The Health and Safety Executive (HSE) has published extensive advice on best practice to minimise stress at work (updates are available on its website). There is much sound advice, however, the emphasis tends to be on cost control and risk management benefits to employers and Human Resources departments. Indeed, perhaps the use of the term "human resources" contributes to the problem, signalling something about the organisational culture to employees that they are resources (things we tend to exploit) rather than individuals (persons for whom we care).

While the benefits to staff in the HSE advice are implicit they are rarely discussed, and the real human suffering that is encountered in the extremes of stress and burnout is often sidelined. This is perhaps the real problem and the focus of this booklet, the suffering of people, not the organisational and financial difficulties. The emphasis on the latter tends to produce guidelines for developing effective systems of control, monitoring and ways of softening the system (like introducing counselling sessions) rather than tackling more difficult and fundamental issues, such as why those who enter caring professions are more prone to stress and burnout in the first place and what part an organisation might be playing in exacerbating the problem.

There is a tendency in organisations to adopt an "illness model" in relation to the employee when burnout arises, and indeed for individuals to accept this approach. The person is made to feel that there is something wrong with him or her rather than the situation in which they find themselves. This permits organisations to perpetuate denial of the problem, adopting simplistic solutions (e.g. providing stress management programmes) which allows the organisation to say it has "done something" without really getting to the root causes. A culture of denial thus avoids the difficulty of facing up to the complexity of burnout and the part it plays in creating and sustaining it. It can be easier to look for some perceived weakness in the employee as the cause rather than take the more challenging and painful course of facing up to the weaknesses in the organisation's values, systems and practices.

Another impact of the illness model is the tendency to reduce the phenomenon to a simplistic, linear symptoms-diagnosis-treatment response. Thus the person who has something "wrong" with him or her can take some time "off sick", perhaps get a prescription for anti-depressants or tranquillisers (burnout is often mistaken for depression, the latter is often an element of burnout but it is not the primary source of struggle) or access to a counsellor and a referral to the occupational health department. This introduces another risk; sick leave with a diagnosis of "stress" may allow a period of respite for some degree of superficial recovery or at least an adjustment in coping mechanisms. The person can return to work apparently less stressed.

Stress tends to disappear once the source such as overwork is removed and the person can have some time away from it. A holiday, for example, can appear to work wonders on our stress levels and we can return to work re-energised and invigorated. Many employers systematically adopt this approach to staff welfare, giving them breaks from the front line until they recuperate then sending them back into the melee once more, to get stressed, take a break, return and so on. Burnout may appear to be helped by such measures but the underlying causality is untouched by stress reduction methods in the long term. Unfinished business may return to haunt the person later. The burned out person is indeed stressed, but the causes lie more deeply than in organisational or personal weaknesses. In burnout, something is going on in work or home that is provoking a breakdown of "normal" ways of coping; something is going on in the person that is summoning up a different way of being in the world, not just doing, but being.

Superficially stress and burnout thus have similar signs and symptoms, but rarely is the picture black and white, not least because stress is often a component in burnout:-

1. In a sense, the symptoms of burnout can be seen as defence mechanisms – a way of shutting down and disengaging when life has become too painful. People who are stressed are caught up in over engagement (although this may precede burnout as we try harder to cope and fix all the problems).
2. In the stressed stage we tend to over-react emotionally, burnout is associated more with feeling numb.
3. Stressed people tend to recover from the emotional and physical trauma once they are able to de-stress. In burnout, the primary wounding is emotional and spiritual and tends to linger even if stress has diminished and physical wellbeing has recovered.
4. The cause of stress can usually be pinpointed and can come and go quickly as the stress source is present or absent. Burnout tends to have a more gradual onset, often the cause is obscure, and gradually worsens until crisis point when the person can barely function at all, even if the apparent cause of the stress is withdrawn.
5. Stress tends to primarily affect physical energy and drive, whilst the emotional and spiritual draining is more a characteristic of burnout.
6. Burnout tends to produce a sense of hopelessness, helplessness, loss of ideals, fear, demoralisation, while the focus of stress is more on disintegration and inability to function.
7. Stress produces a loss of energy and stamina, while burnout produces a feeling of loss like grief as the old self, ways of doing things or accepted norms seem to be dying.
8. Burnout produces a depression rooted in turning inwards to protect oneself, whilst depression with stress is a way of coming to a halt in order to restore energy and vitality.
9. Stressed people tend to become hyperactive and demanding, whereas burnout is associated more with depersonalisation and detachment.
10. Stress is more connected to panic attacks and phobias and possible physical illnesses that may be life threatening. Burnout rarely kills, but may produce feelings that life is not worth living.

Beyond the person and the organisation are the wider cultural aspects which may be affecting burnout rates (see, for example, the research by Tacey or Heelas et al. in the bibliography). Reductionist views that see burnout as a problem of the weak person or organisation and offer stress reduction solutions fail to take account of the bigger picture. For example, Heelas and his colleagues write of the "subjective turn" of the last 50 years or so. Hitherto, a characteristic of our culture was the tendency for people to identify themselves according to objective, externally defined criteria - established ways of doing things, deference to authority, acceptance of certain truths (e.g. the superiority of men, professionals and so on) as givens. The death of defining ourselves in the world in this way is characterised in the subjective turn – a cultural shift where we seek inner understanding and meaning, exploration of self, personal experience of the world and so on. In this model we do not define ourselves or our place in society objectively according to the views of others, but through our own individualist reference points.

The subjective turn has led to changes in organisational emphases. In health, social, educational and other public and pastoral services generally, it was always doctor (or nurse, teacher, minister, social worker etc.) knows best. Now it is patient centred or customer centred care, patient's charters, public rights, partnership and involvement. Surrender to authority is no longer acceptable or desirable if such "customer centred" approaches are implemented. Yet many professional carers find themselves trapped in organisations that do not foster this approach to those they employ, inclining instead to what Heelas and his colleagues have called an "iron cage" model of authoritarianism and bureaucracy. After some time trying to accommodate the iron cage, many give up and go part time, or leave to find some environment more in tune with their subjective needs. Or they burn out in the effort to "do their best" with seemingly impossible demands of "users" before them and indifferent not to say hostile organisations behind them.

Thus the backdrop to burnout is a complicated jig-saw puzzle of many causative factors for which simplistic solutions are unhelpful. From the extensive literature on burnout, and the experiences of organisations like the Sacred Space Foundation, it is possible to see varying degrees of three interweaving primary forces that cultivate burnout:-

1. The person is not in right relationship with the employing organisation, experiencing it as a place of stress, conflict, power struggles, dehumanisation and absence of support. It is not "walking its talk" – ostensibly being some form of caring service, yet not matching this with the response to employees. Practice fails to match values.
2. The person is not in right relationship with colleagues; team relationships tending to mirror the unhealthy relationships of the wider organisation characterised by lack of mutual support, defensiveness, power games and so on.
3. The person may not be in right relationship with him/herself; some aspects of the nature of their work or personal lives may be in conflict with what is healthy for him/her.

Finally, burnout is very much a modern phenomenon and has been studied and described almost exclusively in relatively wealthy, Western societies. Reports of burnout do not seem to arise in less prosperous "third world" societies or aboriginal cultures. These cultures have their own problems, but burnout does not appear to be one of them. It has been particularly observed amongst middle class-professional people, especially those involved in some form of caring work. However, whilst the tendency is for burnout to occur amongst the caring professions as mentioned above, it is not exclusively so. It may be that some people bring very caring qualities into businesses that do not explicitly require caring skills or caring for people, but the person may "care" about the job and get caught up in overgiving all the same. Nevertheless burnout tends predominantly to affect professional carers of all sorts who may be bringing their natural heart-centredness into their jobs. In doing so they seem to get into patterns of over-giving while under–receiving – valuing looking after others but often neglecting to value themselves. One of the solutions to burnout is to move more to patterns of equally valuing the caring of the self, feeding one's own soul as much as that of others. Conversely, unloving people tend not to get burnout, as Dina Glouberman in her fascinating exploration points out, but they do get problems in other ways. Why some people get caught up in over-giving, in controlling or co-dependent relationships in their caring work, in an excessive "neediness" to care and its rewards, why they have difficulty in knowing and maintaining healthy relationships and boundaries for themselves – these are subjects explored a little more later on.

At the Foundation we have found the Enneagram (see Riso and Hudson in the bibliography for a detailed explanation) a particularly useful tool for bringing insight as to why some people are more likely to fall into burnout than others. On balance it does not seem to be restricted to one type of person or occupation, but is more related to how healthy (in a spiritual and psychological sense) the person is, how far they are "at home" in themselves, how far they are in balance and harmony with their inner world and with the world of relationships, roles and work. Where there is disharmony, this is the grist for the mill of the inner work that the person in burnout needs to undertake if they are not to fall into repeating old patters or sinking into victimhood as the "poor me" against the "the big bad employer".

To summarise at this stage:-
1. Burnout and stress are related but different.
2. Burnout occurs predominantly but not exclusively in those involved in caring occupations and situations.

3. It is made worse when its nature is not recognised or misdiagnosed as a mental health problem.

5. It may take many years to gradually emerge.

6. It is more common in organisations which are
   a. ignorant of the processes that produce burnout.
   b. unaware of how to respond to it.
   c. in denial about how their own values and systems play a part.
   d. failing to "walk their talk".
   e. poor in meeting expectations and boundaries in job descriptions, hours of work, opportunities for achievement, support.

7. The caring nature of some persons and lack of awareness of their own inner processes may lead them to be more prone to burnout.

8. Unhealthy relationships between the employee and other team members, with the wider organisation and some inner aspect of the self are more likely to lead to burnout.

2. A spiritual crisis

Burnout may be related to stress in the workplace and the demands of caring, but there are invariably deeper issues at work. The challenge of burnout is to treat it for what it is – a spiritual crisis. Work and caring pressures are factors it is true, but these are often the *agents provocateurs* rather than the root causes. Burnout is the desperate cry of the very essence of who we are/the highest self/the soul to break free. It is symptomatic of a longing to be liberated, no longer defined by who or what others say we are. It is the struggle to be in the world in which we find and give love and compassion; have work and relationships that have heart and meaning for us. It is the longing to be free of old wounds and other unconscious processes that limit our definitions and understanding of ourselves, our freedom to be in the world fully and authentically who we truly are. This struggle for truth and authenticity, when we are trapped in work and relationships that inhibit or edit us and which no longer nurture us, can lead to an experience of profound exhaustion. It is an exhaustion made worse by confusion if we can see no way out, or understand why we feel so bad, or try to help ourselves by injecting even more effort to get things back to "normal".

Spirituality is all about the way each person finds meaning, purpose and connection in the world – how we relate to ourselves, to each other and perhaps (for many people) to an Absolute, God, Ultimate Reality. Spirituality helps us to find our grounding in the world, our purpose for living, to seek and find the answers to questions such as "Who am I?" "Why am I here?" "Where am I going?" and "How do I get there?" Some people find the answers to questions like these in religion, others do not, although everyone seems to seek, that is part of the nature of what it is to be human. Thus on this basis everyone is spiritual but not everyone is religious.

A spiritual crisis is a crisis of meaning, purpose and connection, and so is burnout. Everything that we once thought of as normal or valuable or certain in our lives can suddenly be thrown into turmoil. Psychotherapist and author Frances Vaughan writes that "anyone who has experienced burnout, a common occupational hazard among helping professionals, has probably had the feeling of being trapped in a web of necessity and impossible demands. Most recommended treatments for burnout consist of stress reduction or setting boundaries. They overlook the fact that burnout usually indicates a state of spiritual aridity, and the effective treatment may call for spiritual renewal or awakening the soul."

This "spiritual aridity" is burnout. It is what happens when the energy we are investing in trying to keep things "normal", to keep control of our lives, to keep things the same becomes more and more demanding. As the energy required to keep things stable increases, we become increasingly depleted, exhausted and heartsick with the effort. The greater the exhaustion the closer we get to an almost complete state of mental, physical, social and spiritual collapse. At some level one or more relationships is changing, or change is being demanded, perhaps with work, a primary personal relationship or with our deepest truth about ourselves and our beliefs. Often the process is an unconscious one as we call to ourselves challenge after challenge that brings us closer to the edge, even though consciously we may think we do not want these things to be happening. Things seem to fall apart despite our best efforts – one thing after another goes wrong. We may feel that the cause lies in something outside ourselves – a bullying boss, new demands on us at work but without the resources to meet them, a relationship at home that has grown cold, the demands of a loved one for care, a sudden trauma in life that throws all our cherished values into question. While these external factors are indeed happening, and we may project the cause of our distress onto them, something deeper may be at work.

This account from an Anglican minister summarises one person's feelings about burnout; Luke (not his real name) wrote:-

"Last year my body, mind and soul started playing up. I was slow to ask for help; those around me tried to help, and for a while things seemed all right. However life was not normal. Bit by bit everything was falling apart. I was slow starting in the morning. I had no concentration, and the slightest pressure tipped the balance. Emotional breakdown, "burnout", followed. At one point I described it as the worst thing I had ever experienced, although I wasn't to know it would get worse still. I appealed to my maker, but there was silence. Silence, I guess, because I was unable to listen."

Burnout is a form of deep human suffering at every level (physical, psychological, social and spiritual) which occurs when old ways of being in the world no longer work and disintegrate. Disease (dis-ease) in many forms can occur; a few can become so distressed as the pressure mounts that severe physical or mental illness or even suicide can result. The suffering is accentuated because the cause is not clear to us, although we may project it onto external events, but these are only the mirror to our inner unconscious processes. It is also made worse because our usual resources for dealing with such distress do not seem to work and there seems no way out of what appears to be a spiralling, downward struggle demanding more and more effort just to keep functioning; these demands in turn fuelling the burning out, the loss of energy at every level. Stuck in our present way of being we may find we cannot look up or beyond and see how things might be otherwise, or the dream of how things might be but seems so out of reach just adds the frustration and sense of stuckness. The vision of a life without suffering eludes us, so we can become immobilised – unable to move to the future while struggling frantically to hold to the painful present.

It is like being far out to sea in a small boat, the familiar harbour has been left behind and no amount of frantic rowing seems to get us any closer to getting back there, meanwhile, over the horizon there may be a new safe haven, but it is invisible to us and its existence thereby doubted.

Nothing less than a complete transformation in our way of being is arising and, whether we perceive it consciously or whether it is bubbling along in the unconscious, this too can be terrifying. The levels of fear, panic, pain and distress in our lives are often unprecedented.

Some respond by becoming a victim of circumstance; a response where we tell ourselves that bad things happen and there is little or nothing we can do except surrender, fight back or try to maintain the status quo. Struggling to keep going in the face of what seems like an attack can be immensely energy intensive, leading to the collapse known as burnout. In this model, we are victims and other than engaging in the fight, perhaps by getting the trade union on our "side" or blaming a loved one, there are limits to what we can do.

Another approach is to try to change things in the workplace or home. At work employers might bring in counselling opportunities, or we might take a holiday or distract ourselves with the thought that a change of job or house would help. Attempts like these are a bit like moving the deckchairs around on the Titanic. They provide temporary distraction but do nothing to tackle the underlying problem. Any relief is always temporary.

Burnout is therefore always a call for change. Here are some vignettes of individual experiences:-

John: a dentist who spent a lot of his life doing things to meet with the approval of others, including the career path his parents wanted for him. He realised that all his life he'd been a dentist because that was what his parents wanted. His work had become a burden to him, some days he could not start the car to set off there. Healing things in himself around his parents, he left dentistry and became a meditation teacher and is very happy.

Julia: a woman locked in a relationship where she could not be true to herself and had spent decades to the point of exhaustion trying to stay with what she deemed socially acceptable. For her, becoming whole and accepted in the world meant that she had to face up her true self and to the difficulties of telling her family and partner about her sexuality that she had kept under wraps all these years. Burnout tends to persist when we will not, or cannot, move.

Gina: who had given her best as a nurse, always willing to go the extra mile, to work through her breaks, do the overtime, anything to please the patient. She often said "I am a nurse", identified strongly with the role and was devastated when in quick succession a patient complained about her and she was made aware of the possibility of redundancy.

Michael: a Roman Catholic priest who felt alone in his difficult parish, torn between the relentless demands of his parishioners, the expectations of himself and his parents, the feeling that he had to make everything in the church right, the lack of support from the church authorities. When he finally plucked up courage to ask for help was told by his bishop that there must be something wrong with him. His faith was shattered, he felt God had abandoned him and even doubted the reality of God. Eventually a spiritual director/counsellor was found for him but he was told that it would be months for an appointment and was meanwhile told that daily prayer would solve the problem. Eventually, through a process of reconnection with the Divine which was long and sometime painful, he found a new place for himself in the world and the church.

Graham: a fire officer, who had been leading his team and had many years of experience in his job seeing the worst of things that could happen to human beings; doing his best to keep all the team supported in the horrors they encountered. Passed over for promotion, witnessing the effects of a particularly terrible house fire, divorced and stuck in an unhappy relationship, a chronic health problem, struggling to maintain his relationship with his children – he became unable to function at work, sullen, angry and indifferent to the needs of others. These unhealthy ways of cutting himself off from demands led him into further disciplinary trouble with his employer.

Lisa: a teacher, found herself unable to cope with her class. The children seemed to ask more and more of her. Reorganisation of the school made her feel like targets and examination successes were more important than the development of the children. Her values were increasingly in conflict with the school's values. The head teacher, also harassed and under pressure, placed more and more pressure on Lisa to conform. She felt bullied, went "off sick", but felt she had no one to turn to for help and the longer she was away from work the more difficult the thought of returning.

Geoff: a social worker, felt trapped by his job. He had come to hate the work, felt that the clients were ever ready to attack him or complain or place new demands on him. He longed to escape and go to college to do that degree in art he had always wanted to do, to work in ways that were creative and inspiring. His wife was dependent on him, he had children to feed, money had to be earned to pay the bills and keep a roof over their heads. With each day he felt more and more trapped, that he was in the "wrong" place but could see no way out because of his responsibilities.

Maria: a manger in a care home, felt overburdened by responsibility. She found it almost impossible to delegate. After a complaint she would have sleepless nights wondering what was happening in the home in her absence. She tended to get involved with all the decisions in the home, would not allow or indeed trust others to help and found herself having intensifying feelings that she must manage things alone, must be in charge, must "do it, because if I don't know one else will or can".

These examples illuminate many of the primary factors associated with burnout:-

Disconnection with the goals, values, practices of the working environment.
Feeling powerless, exhausted and overwhelmed by caring responsibilities.
Feeling undervalued, unseen, unrecognised, unsupported, under attack.
Feeling alone and disconnected from colleagues and other sources of help.
Feeling disconnected from ourselves, what has heart and meaning for us and sources of help including God.
Getting caught up in patterns of overgiving with a lack of personal boundaries.
Wanting to control everything at work and within ourselves.
Life becoming dominated by feelings of fear and anxiety rather than love and fulfilment.

3. Self assessment

At this point you might consider your response to the following to see if there are risk factors in your own life that are making burnout a possibility for you. Have a look at each statement and answer yes or no according to whether you agree with them. Treat a maybe or a "not sure" as a no. The questions are not designed as tricks or to be definitive, but intended to explore the general trends that may be at work in you, what your working environment is like, its feel-good factor, and also about how you see yourself in this – what value you place on yourself and your ability/opportunity to take care of yourself. There's no need to get too analytical about them, and often it's best just to trust your initial response and go with that. Some of the questions may not apply directly to your situation, so just answer the ones you can.

Then total your "yes" score in each group. Group A looks at your relationship to your work, what it feels like in your wider employing organisation. Group B focuses more on what relationships are like in your immediate team or workmates. Group C asks you to look at some factors about how you are relating to and taking care of yourself. These statements are taken from the topic areas of discussion that are part of our work with individuals and groups at the Foundation.

A. Relationships with the wider employing organisation as a whole:-
1. I know what is expected of me.
2. I have sufficient resources to do the job.
3. I have the opportunity to do what I do best.
4. I have received praise from my boss in the last seven days.
5. I am aware of what is going on in the organisation.
6. I can participate in decisions that affect my work.
7. My boss has talked with me about my progress within the last six months.
8. I would recognise all the executives of the organisation (e.g. Chief executive and others) if I saw them.
9. What I have to say counts.
10. I have the support and opportunity to keep learning.
11. This is a great organisation to work for.
12. I feel the organisation cares about me.

B. Relationships with your immediate team – the group of people you work with on a regular basis:-
1. Although our work is serious and hard, my team laughs easily and plays hard too.
2. I feel able to ask my team for help when I need it.
3. In my team, people offer help without needing to be asked.

4. I trust my team to keep a confidence about me.
5. Work is a pleasure with this team.
6. We talk about our work and reflect on it to make it better, in formal sessions, at least monthly.
7. We have pre-shift and post shift debriefings to check that everyone arrives and leaves work feeling OK.
8. We have at least one day a year as a team out of the work situation where as many as possible of us gather to review how we work together and see how we might improve our relationships.
9. I feel confident that my team does not gossip about me when my back is turned.
10. I do not gossip about my team members in their absence.
11. I feel respected in my team.
12. I have the opportunity to take "5" and gather myself without being made to feel guilty or shamed.

C. Relationships with yourself – taking care of "me":-
1. I get a good night's sleep.
2. I eat a healthy, well-balanced diet.
3. I take plenty of exercise.
4. I can talk through work problems with my partner/a close friend.
5. Work does not interfere with my personal time.
6. Other people's problems at work don't get to me.
7. I practice some form of meditation or relaxation regularly.
8. I can withdraw appropriately if a situation at work gets too stressful.
9. I have a day a month when I do exactly as I please.
10. I allow myself a good read, or something similar, every day, for at least half an hour that takes all of my attention and is nothing to do with work.
11. I make sure I get my proper breaks for meals and refreshments at work.
12. I know my limits and boundaries and I keep to them.

How did you score? There's no fixed right or wrong result, but in general the fewer "yes" answers you have for each one the higher the risks to yourself. If you score 100% in any of these you are probably kidding yourself or you are in denial! Most people who are OK in their lives and work will get around 75%. If you are scoring 50% "yes" answers or less in any of the above lists there is cause for concern, indicating a higher risk that burnout is on the cards for you unless you take action. Sometimes we can score highly in one whilst others are weak. It may be that if you are very solid in yourself (Group C questions) then you are able to deal very well with a negative employing organisation and/or team, but on balance, low scores should be seen as wake up calls demanding attention. The risks would be incrementally greater if the score is below

50% in more than one of these. Conversely, each question has an implicit answer. So, for example, if you have answered 'no' to question 2 in Group C, are there steps you can take to improve the way you look after yourself with a better diet? It is important not to get into trying to get a high score on all of them at once if there is a problem. Putting that degree of energy into it will probably make things worse! Be gentle on yourself. If there are problem areas, set one or two realistic goals rather than trying to sort the whole lot out. For example, in Group A you may have felt that you do not have the power to change a lot of things, but you might be able to fix an appointment with your boss to talk about your progress or ask for help. Or it may be that some things in Group A are beyond you, but you can reduce your risks by boosting your score in another arena, e.g. in Group B you might look at what can be done to develop better working relationships in your team.

Now take a look at the next questionnaire, which can be thought of as a self diagnostic tool – "How close am I to burnout?" These statements apply to your life in general, including work and home. Once again, don't try picking away at them and analysing, just allow your responses to surface spontaneously and for an overall picture to emerge and answer "yes" or "no" to each.

1. I find myself feeling stressed or irritated when others make even simple demands of me.
2. Work always seems to exhaust me.
3. I seem to get angry more easily than I used to.
4. I have this feeling of being in the "wrong" place a lot of the time.
5. I worry about things a lot more than I used to.
6. When I go to sleep, I wake up feeling tired.
7. I often can't sleep because of thoughts/worries racing through my mind.
8. I don't feel a sense of peace.
9. I feel disconnected from normal life.
10. Everybody seems to be OK but me.
11. I seem to move from one job to another and nothing really satisfies.
12. I seem to move from one relationship to another and nothing really satisfies.
13. I feel stuck and going nowhere in my current main relationship(s)
14. I feel stuck and going nowhere in my work.
15. I am more suspicious of people than I used to be.
16. I feel unhappy a lot at home.
17. Work no longer satisfies me.
18. I feel weighed down by responsibility.
19. Changes or demands at work feel like a threat.
20. I feel I'm in the wrong job.

21. I feel I'm in the wrong marriage/partnership.
22. People seem to be avoiding me.
23. I avoid other people.
24. I feel helpless at work.
25. I feel helpless at home.
26. I seem to be running just to stay still – doing more but achieving less.
27. I seem to be helping everyone else, but no-one seems to see my suffering.
28. I get sick a lot.
29. I seem to get a lot of aches and pains.
30. The thought of going to work makes me feel sick.
31. The thought of going home makes me feel sick.
32. Doing ordinary things like shopping seems to take a monumental effort.
33. I seem to forget things more than usual.
34. Normal conversation seems to take more effort than usual.
35. I feel ashamed that I am not coping.
36. I feel no one really understands what life is like for me.
37. People trying to help just make things worse.
38. The future seems hopeless.
39. I've lost confidence in myself.
40. I feel like I'm on my own.
41. Whatever's wrong, it's all my fault.
42. Whatever's wrong, it's because others are getting at me.
43. Things I once believed in don't seem true any more.
44. The world seems a place of horror and despair.
45. I've sometimes thought that death would be better than life.
46. I'm taking more time off work than I used to.
47. At work, I feel like I am under attack a lot of the time.
48. I burst into tears for no apparent reason.
49. I have inexplicable feelings of deep sadness.
50. I can explode with anger at things I would once see as trivial.
51. When I'm talking with people, it's sometimes like we're using different languages.
52. I've lost interest in my pastimes or hobbies.
53. I seem to be making a lot more mistakes than usual.
54. People I love seem to be getting more angry with me.
55. There seems to be no time for anything but work.
56. I've no time for people, even those I love.
57. I seem to indulge in more drink, drugs, food, casual sex, junk TV or whatever.
58. I feel exhausted and drained of energy a lot of the time.
59. At home, people's demands on me can feel like an attack.
60. I feel mentally paralysed and don't know which way to turn.

61. I've lost interest in sex.
62. I spend more time in bed than usual.
63. When things go wrong I tend to blame me.
64. I've put on/lost weight.
65. I've had more of the following of late – headaches, vomiting, diarrhoea, tummy ache, constipation, breathlessness, fainting, dizziness.
66. I seem to be making a lot of mistakes with even the simplest of things.
67. I'm easily irritated by things I would normally ignore – background noises, people speaking, loud TV etc.
68. I seem to be taking more careless risks e.g. at work, while driving, household jobs etc.
69. I've become more cynical.
70. I feel a lot of the time like I just want to curl up in a ball and the world to go away.

This is also taken from the subject areas we use at the Foundation when exploring individual burnout and the kind of responses people report. In general, a "yes" score of 50% or more would indicate a state of serious challenge in your life. More than 75% and you are probably in burnout right now. But these are very general perspectives based on our experience at the Foundation. There is no fixed score, but clearly the higher the number of "yes" answers in this case the closer you are to being in burnout. On balance getting more than 50% "yes" would suggest that you are very close to if not actually in burnout and this is a wake up call to see what needs to be done about it.

Remember that it's the overall picture with these scores that counts rather than responses to individual questions. And the intention of the whole is to raise awareness of the situation so that things can change if needs be.

4. What doesn't help

In our efforts to respond to burnout, some things can be ruled out as unhelpful:-

"Job's comforters" – people telling us constantly that it will be all right, or making endless suggestions for change.

Others who get involved in our drama, no matter how well intentioned, and try to interfere with work or relationships or get angry or upset on our behalf.

Being made to feel like there is something "wrong" with us, by employers or others.

Trying to disconnect from work and people, this just makes us feel lonely and isolated, the problem doesn't go away, we just stew on it more in our isolation.

Escape routes (job or relationship hopping, holidays, the grass is greener phenomenon, alcohol, shopping etc.) may offer temporary respite, but the real issue simply lurks away underneath waiting for the right moment to surface again

Pretending it's not really happening and that it will all go away if the thing/person that is "causing" the problem goes away.

Diagnosis as a psychiatric problem, which sometimes happens because the symptoms may be solely attributable to depression, can again make matters worse by missing what is really going on and locking us into the mental health system with a diagnostic label that may disadvantage us for a long time. Only treating the depressive part of burnout may inhibit awareness and resolution of the deeper underlying difficulties.

Drugs such as antidepressants might get us through the immediate crisis and can be helpful in the short term, but in the long term they may just mask the cause of the suffering which at some point will have to be dealt with.

Trying to "hold it together" and "keep going" – the energy we have to put into doing so exacerbates the exhaustion.

Trying to cope with it all ourselves, to handle it alone. Help is needed and indeed the willingness to embrace help is a sign that the person is ready to recover.

One of the underlying drivers of burnout is the longing to connect at some deep level – with our deepest self, our heart's desire, with others, with the Sacred. There is a paradox here; within our needs to disconnect from work or from people is the underpinning desire to connect more deeply, more meaningfully. In the interim there is a need to withdraw in order to discover what the new forms of connection might be.

5. How to deal with burnout when it happens – the "R" words

Luke's story, mentioned previously, illustrates what it feels like to be in burnout. He went on to write of what helped him out of the "silence":-

"Silence, I guess, because I was unable to listen. One phrase got through. A small card my daughter sent me. It simply said 'You are loved'. Many knowledgeable people got to work: doctor, counsellors, friends and family, spiritual directors; there was a retreat and several useful books: all prescribing lots of rest and exercise, time to think and even space to do absolutely nothing. I hope I never go through that experience again. I trust I have learned some lessons, that the right changes are being made within me and that I will be a more complete person as a result. But whatever the outcome, above all it is good to know 'You are loved.'"

As this story suggests, an immediate task is to get out of the situation - as happens with the people who come into the Foundation's retreat facilities. Or it might be necessary to take "sick leave" or move to the home of a friend or other space where we feel safe and taken care of. Seeking support from a GP is helpful (bearing in mind the limitations mentioned above of getting a diagnosis of depression) not least because the GP can help us to see aspects that we might not see ourselves. A GP aware of burnout will be able to offer suggestions such as those below. He or she can help with authorising sickness leave to cover time off work if necessary and medication as a temporary aide (if, for example, depression is part of the struggle) so that we become more grounded and able to see more clearly what is going on and ways out of it.

On balance, this is not a time for action or trying to make solutions happen – the effort to do these can make the burnout worse; this is a time to come to stillness, to wait and see, to get out of the situation and find the space to allow the solutions that are waiting within to emerge. Thus:-
Retreat - There are lots of possibilities, but getting temporarily out of the unhealthy context and creating the space (the sacred space – where there is time for ourselves which allows the new insights and healings to emerge) for the next steps is a priority.
Rest, Re-energise, Recuperate - looking after our physical wellbeing by eating, exercising and sleeping better are part of the process, coupled with time to reflect on what is going on with ourselves.
Reconnection - this problem cannot be solved alone, despite often very strong feelings otherwise. Disconnection in retreat is not the answer, reconnection is what is called for, so the support of a wise counsellor who can guide us through the reflective process is essential. Birthing within us what needs to come forth is unsafe alone – we need a "spiritual midwife", one or more, to accompany us through this phase.

Recollection, Reflection, Re-visioning - as we recollect what has gone on, we can start a process of re-visioning our lives. Using all kinds of reflective, insight and awareness building processes, such as guided meditation, the Enneagram, inspiring literature, prayer, spiritual direction and so on (more details if desired on all these processes can be found in the books by Wright 2009 and Wright and Sayre-Adams 2009 detailed in the bibliography). Thus we can begin to return to that place in ourselves where we feel at home.

Recovery, Right relationship - a sense of meaning, purpose and connection in life – the very stuff of spirituality. It may become clear to us through this process what has to change in our lives – a different career, a renewal or letting go of a relationship and often and most especially learning to live our lives with what has heart and meaning for us with a deeper connection to our spiritual needs. As we burnout we tend to "hang on" to normality as best we can, or struggle to "go back" to the way things were (There is no going back, our bodies, souls, hearts and minds will not permit it!). One of the signs of a healthy recovery can be our willingness to let go of something – a relationship or a job, for example, that we have been working so hard to stay with. Equally, we may find that the re-visioning process enables us to stay with a job or relationship, because something in ourselves has changed, some change of consciousness or awareness that helps us to be in relationship to ourselves and others in new and less harmful ways.

As we begin to get clearer about what has been happening to us, and what we need to do/how we need to be, an ongoing plan is necessary to ensure we do not slip backwards. Renewal through burnout is about re-birthing ourselves into the world, about living more authentically with what has heart and meaning for us, living from a place of essence, of soul. Four "soul care" key things (addressed in more detail in the book "Coming Home" – see bibliography) need to be in place:-

Soul Friends - access to the support of one or more wise counsellors or mentors to whom we can turn for ongoing guidance when needed in our lives. People who have walked the path before us and know how to support us in times of need.

Soul Communities – groups of people with whom we feel at home and who nourish our ongoing spiritual awakening. It might be a fellow group of meditators, a reflective practice group at work, a church group, a temporary community we encounter during a course that nourishes us, a yoga group and so on, there are many possibilities.

Soul Foods – through the inspiration of poetry, music, art, nature, scripture and so on that refresh, renew and revitalise us.

Soul works - developing spiritual practices which nourish and keep us "at home" in ourselves – meditation, prayer, yoga, retreat time, tai chi, and so on: the list is endless; practical things we can do, some alone, some in groups with our soul community, that help to keep us centred and to nourish right relationship at every level.

Ultimately the crisis of burnout, which is always a spiritual crisis, teaches us much about ourselves, about the limits and boundaries we need to have, about humility – that we do not and cannot be in charge of everything. Healing from burnout we come to acknowledge those things that nourish and stir the heart and soul, what we need to deepen our connection with ourselves and others and perhaps that which lies beyond the self, an Ultimate Reality, God however we experience it. It is commonly reported that the crisis of burnout teaches us something about our relationship with the Ultimate, the Absolute, God. He, She or It has many names and in these individualist times there is a great wariness of all-encompassing theories or religions and hesitancy over the "God" word, but for most people burnout brings them to a place of renewed relationship with the Divine, a relationship that is not distorted by old projections or misunderstandings. Discovering through burnout that we are essentially loved and lovable as we are (and yes that might include, indeed does for most people, finding that deep and abiding love in the very source of the creation itself), that we are worthy of being here and that this love and worthiness does not demand that we be some other's ideas of perfection that we have absorbed, anything other than who we truly are. The journey through burnout is to come to a deep place of knowing our inherent loving nature, to love ourselves as ourselves; for many that is coming to know that we are absolutely loved by the Beloved. Resting in that place of love of ourselves, by ourselves and perhaps our God, we can learn to let go of the need to be in control, to always please others, to make impossible demands on ourselves and instead be who we truly are and true to ourselves in the world – at Home.

6. Prevention

If we refer again to the self assessment questions in Groups A-C of part 3, each of these statements offers some clues about what needs to change. However, it is important to be gentle on ourselves and remember that we do not have to have everything perfectly in place (trying to be perfect or make the world perfect is one of the catalysts for burnout!). The trick is to adopt an incremental approach – the more bits of the jig saw puzzle are in place the more complete the picture, but it does not have to be done all at once. For example, it may not be possible to do much about the wider workplace culture, but could something be done, such as implementing reflective practice, to enhance support in the team? Could we do something to improve our diet or ensure we have a day a month of "me" time? Starting small first by tackling one or two achievable issues than can make a difference is a more realistic and healthy approach.

Preventing burnout or preventing a recurrence (and it can return if we stray from being in right relationship) can follow similar lines. Looking at the statements in the first three groups some of the answers lie there – such as finding better ways to take care of ourselves, building better teams, and creating more hospitable employment environments, such as those recommended by the Health and Safety Executive. If burnout is a sign of soul sickness, then bringing things into the workplace which make our working relationships more soulful – replete with meaning, connection and purpose - would appear to be helpful. If we look at the work of Hatfield, Goleman, Zohar, Wright and Sayre-Adams and others, some common threads can be seen. Workplaces that feed the soul and are spiritually and emotionally inspiring, connected and meaningful, rooted in right relationship at every level are more likely to be happier, healthier and more productive places to be, to have less sickness, absenteeism, stress and burnout and have higher levels of staff and user satisfaction. Why? Because the staff in such places, such teams, feel more supportive of each other, have a shared sense of mission and purpose in their work and a deeper sense of connection with each other (and perhaps that which is beyond the other) which makes the work culture more soulful, more satisfying. Dis-spirited workforces are a recipe for disaster for the individuals who work in them, for the teams and for those who depend on them for care.

Suggestions for improving workplace and caring relationships, for building more connected and soulful communities and connections, are wide ranging. The many studies cited in the bibliography include possibilities such as:-
Effective systems for monitoring care needs and workloads and ensuring adequate resources and support are in place.
Access to support and self help groups with shared interests.
Setting up shared educational programmes that cross professional boundaries.

Social events that bring people together.

Multidisciplinary projects that help people work across their usual boundaries and understand each others' contributions.

Time out days, sabbaticals, retreats, time set aside as respite sessions from caring for others..

Pre and post work shift de-briefings that help people deal with issues that are causing them difficulty before they start work and before they leave.

Team building sessions, away from the work setting.

Developing and implementing anti-bullying policies.

Networking and learning sets with groups with similar interests.

Using email networks, staff journals etc. to ensure everyone knows what's going on.

Staff involvement in decision making at every level.

Stress management education.

Time and support for developing and pursuing interests not necessarily connected to work.

Introducing relaxation techniques for employees such as meditation training, tai chi, complementary therapies etc.

Creating quiet "sanctuaries" where employees can be in silence away from work.

Access to independent counselling.

Leadership development.

Clear job descriptions illustrating reasonable expectations and boundaries.

These are just a few examples of the many possibilities available and which have been used with some success according to the reports in a wide range of settings. What is needed, if the extremes of stress and burnout are to be prevented, is a comprehensive strategy, not just providing employee friendly policies or staff counselling or team building days or better personal exercise, but "and." It is all of these and more – the more comprehensive and focussed the strategy, the more it is likely to be successful in prevention. A root and branch approach seems necessary at every level of the organisation and in individuals to produce a culture that is inclusive, supportive and nurturing. The cultivation of right relationships between the organisation and those it employs and serves, among teams, and the individual employees sense of being in right relationship with the self are key levels of concern. The interplay of the relationships between the individual person's inner experience (which will include for most people a deepening of the relationship with their higher self or the Divine, however they experience this) and how we feel about ourselves, how grounded, "at one", at home in ourselves we are, the quality of relationships in teams and the wider organisation – all these provide the milieu for burnout to arise or not. Thus prevention of burnout takes place at many different levels simultaneously, for it could be argued that all the staff and carer support policies in the world will not help if a person is not in right relationship with him/herself. Equally, it is a tough call to expect an individual to carry through the inner exploration of moving to right relationship with the self if the burden of caring is overwhelming or working relationships are out of balance.

However, there is a paradox here. It seems, like motherhood and apple pie, that preventing burnout is self-evidently good. Yet, if we look at the evidence cited of those who have passed through burnout, one of the outcomes is that people tend to be grateful for it – Glouberman talks of the "joy" of burnout and Wright and Sayre-Adams of the "awakening to our bliss, our sacred truth". With the benefit of hindsight (and it may be many years later that this process of healing and forgiveness reaches this stage) we can come to see that although it was terrible at the time, without burnout we would not have transformed our lives into new and more meaningful, authentic, loving and heart-warming ways. We would not have come to a place of being at home in ourselves to find deeper joy in loving relationships at every level, perhaps the Divine too. It could be argued that burnout should not be prevented if this is the case! On the other hand, perhaps there are also ways of finding a more soulful path in life without going through the torment of burnout.

Although burnout is a terribly painful experience it is also pregnant with potential for leading a happier, truthful and more fulfilling life. Those who are in burnout and those who help them might do well to bear this in mind. It may be difficult, if not impossible, to embrace this message especially in the early stages, but at some point, in the words of mother Julian of Norwich, "all shall be well" – and therein there is hope.

7. Support for others

Thus far the emphasis has been on the needs of the person in burnout, but others need support too. Enlightened employers can make sure that the person's absence from work is allowed to take its course, that there is no pressure to return. One way of ensuring the latter is to make certain the person has clear space and absence of connection with work issues and colleagues. The remaining team may need to have extra help brought in to cope with the workload so that they too are not put under pressure. They need to be kept up to date with developments, have clear reasons why it is best to leave the person alone and to be wary of falling into being Job's comforters or feeling that they must act to help.

Families and friends can feel confused by the person's responses – sometimes it manifests as withdrawal (physical, emotional), anger, unwillingness to engage in everyday conversation or make plans. Close friends, spouses and partners can be especially hurt by the disconnection of their loved one, by their sense of impotence to help someone they love who is clearly suffering, the apparent unwillingness of the person to follow requests or accept offers of help. Carers, especially partners, spouses and children need guidance about what is happening to the one they love, how best to support them, and they will need supporters in turn – a friendly confidante, some private time, other interests to pursue, a counsellor, someone who knows about the subject to advise them on what to do/not to do, support groups and so on. The loved ones of the person in burnout can find themselves under great strain as they try to cope, and close personal relationships can be stretched to the limits. The supporters need support too.

8. Endpoints

Finally, a few important points to remember:-

1. Burnout is not a fixed condition, it is a transient and it will pass.
2. Burning out does not mean that we cannot re-ignite and find new passion and zeal in our lives.
3. It is not a social or physical or psychological problem, though all the symptoms are demonstrated in these domains.
4. It is a spiritual problem – a crisis of meaning and purpose in life, when the deepest core of our being simply cannot bear to be in the world without being true to itself.
5. It is a crisis of disconnection from old ways of being and the hunger for new, more meaningful ways of connection.
6. It is not a dead end, but an opportunity for learning and transformation.
7. The "causes" are often seen as external factors (the unloving partner, the threat of redundancy, the difficult boss etc.) but these are invariably catalysts for something that is going on deep within ourselves.
8. Just because you have burned out once does not mean it cannot happen again. Unless we maintain a consistent pattern of self care and awareness it is easy to "forget", to get caught up in old patterns. However, experience suggests that once we start to feel off centre and disconnected again, we are more likely to recognise the symptoms and take corrective action.
9. Burnout is a wake up call, the demand from our deepest source to find our true path in life.
10. Approaching burnout from a spiritual perspective does not obviate the need for good employment practices or excuse abusive behaviour or the need to access medical and other therapeutic sources of help. The spiritual, holistic perspective is not either/or but embraces an inclusive approach of tackling the challenge using all effective possibilities.

9. Bibliography and suggested further reading

Ammon L 2005 Burnout in Long-term Care Social Work www.friedsocialworker.com/Articles/longtermcareburnout. htm

Belmonte D 2009 Teaching from the Deep End: Succeeding with Today's Classroom Challenges. Corwin. London

Blyth G 2006 Reclothed in our rightful mind. Signs of the Times/Modern Church people's Union. 23: Oct

Borrill C, Wall T, West M, Hardy G et al 1998 Mental Health of the Workforce in NHS Trusts. Institute of Work Psychology. University of Sheffield

Cherniss C 1980 Staff Burnout: Job Stress in the Human Services. Sage. Beverly Hills

Cole T, Carlin N 2009 The Suffering of Physicians. Lancet. 374(9699):1414-5.

Confederation of British Industry (CBI) 1999 Promoting Mental Health at Work. CBI. London

Cordeiro W 2009 Leading on Empty. Bethany. London

Demerouti E, Verbeke W and Bakker A 2005 Exploring the Relationship Between a Multidimensional and Multifaceted Burnout Concept and Self-Rated Performance. Journal of Management 31 (2) 186-209

Dollard M, Winefield A and Winefield H 2003 Occupational Stress in the Service Professions. Taylor and Francis. London

Dunham J and Varma V (eds.) 1998 Stress in Teachers: Past, Present and Future. Whurr. London

Freudenberger H and Richelson G 1980 Burnout: The High Cost of High Achievement. Doubleday. New York

Glouberman D 2002 The Joy of Burnout; how the end of the world can be a new beginning. Hodder Mobius. London

Goleman D 1995 Emotional Intelligence. Bantam. New York.

Gooding L 2005 Stress Poses Dire Threat to NHS. Nursing Standard 19 (21) 4

Greenberg J 1999 Comprehensive Stress Management. McGraw-Hill. Boston

Grosch W and Olsen D 2000 Clergy burnout: an integrative approach. J Clin Psychol. 56 (5) 619-32

Gunn B 2004 The Antidote to Burnout. Strategic Finance 86 (3) 8-10

Harden R 2007 What price priesthood? Church Times Issue 7508 2 February

Hatfield D 1999 Gallup Organisation: new research links emotional intelligence with profitability. The Inner Edge 1(5) 5-9

Health Education Authority 1996 Organisational Stress. HEA. London

Health Education Authority 1998 More Than Brown Bread and Aerobics. HEA. London

Health and Safety Executive 2009 Data from Website www.hse.gov.uk/statistics/pdf

Heelas P and Woodhead l, with Seel B, Szerszynski B, Tusting K 2005 The Spirituality Revolution – why religion is giving way to spirituality. Blackwell. Oxford

Kaldor P and Bullpitt R 2001 Burnout in church leaders. Openbook. Adelaide

Kansas State University 2009 Burnout Among Police Officers: differences in how male and female police officers manage stress may accentuate stress on the job. ScienceDaily http://www.sciencedaily.com / releases/2009/02/090226110651.htm

Kirwan M and Armstrong D 1995 Investigation of Burnout in a Sample of British General Practitioners. Br J Gen Pract. 45(394):259-60.

Kyriacou C 2001 Teacher Stress: Directions for Future Research. Educational Review 53 (1) 28-35

Lehr F 2006 Clergy Burnout: Recovering From The 70 Hour Week and Other Self-defeating Practices Fortress. Minneapolis

Libby B 1987 Understanding and Managing Stress in the Academic World. CCPS. Ann Arbor

Long M, Meyer D and Jacobs G 2007 Psychological Distress Among American Red Cross Disaster Workers Responding to the Terrorist Attacks of September 11 2001. Psychiatry Research 149: 303-308

Maslach C 1982 Burnout - The Cost of Caring. Prentice-Hall. New York

Maslach C and Jackson S 1986 Maslach Burnout Inventor. Consulting Psychologists Press. Palo Alto

Maslach C and Leiter P 1997 The Truth About Burnout: How Organizations Cause Personal Stress and What to Do About It. Jossey-Bass. San Francisco

Mateen F and Dorji C 2009 Health-care worker burnout and the mental health imperative. Lancet. 22;374(9690):595-7.

McConnel E 1982 Burnout in the Nursing Profession. Mosby. St. Louis

McFarlane C 2004 Risks Associated with the Psychological Adjustment of Humanitarian Aid Workers. Australasian Journal of Disaster 1:1-16

McManus I, Winder B and Gordon D 2002 The causal links between stress and burnout in a longitudinal study of UK doctors. Lancet 2002, 359:2089-2090

McManus I, Keeling A and Paice E 2004 Stress, Burnout and Doctors' Attitudes to Work Are Determined by Personality and Learning Style: A twelve year longitudinal study of UK medical graduates. Department of Psychology, University College London. London

Moore D and Moore J 1996 Posthurricane Burnout: an island township's experience. Environment and Behaviour (January) 134-155

Morris H 2000 The long war against God. Master. New York

Pennachio D 2005 Burnout: Are you at risk? Medial Economics 78-82 May 6th

Read G 2009 Ministry Burnout. Grove. Cambridge

Riso D and Hudson R 1999 Wisdom of the Enneagram. Bantam. New York

Routledge C and Francis L 2005   Burnout among male Anglican parochial clergy in England: testing a modified form of the Maslach Burnout Inventory. Research in the Social Scientific Study of Religion 15: 71-94

Sanford J 1982 Ministry Burnout. Paulist. Minneapolis

Schaefer F, Blazer D, Carr K, Connor K, Burchett B, Schaefer C, et al. 2007 Traumatic Events and Posttraumatic Stress in Cross-Cultural Mission Assignments. Journal of Traumatic Stress 20 (4) 529-539

(The) Society of Mary and Martha 2003 Affirmation and Accountability. SMM. Dunsford

Snow C and Willard P 1989 I'm Dying to Take Care of You. Professional Counsellor Books. Redmond

Tacey D 2003 The Spiritual Revolution. Harpercollins. Sydney

Tomic W and Evers W 2004 A Question of Burnout Among Reformed Church Ministers in The Netherlands. Mental Health, Religion & Culture 7 (3) 225–247

UNHCR HQ Staff Welfare Unit, Career and Staff Support Service 2001 Managing the Stress of Humanitarian Emergencies Geneva UNHCR

Vaughan F 1995 Shadows of the Sacred. Quest. Wheaton

Williams S, Mitchie S, Pattani S 1998 Improving the Health of the NHS Workforce. Nuffield. London

Wood T and McCarthy C 2002 Understanding and Preventing Teacher Burnout. CTTE. Washington

World Health Organisation 1994 Guidelines for the Primary Prevention of Mental, Neurological and Psychosocial Disorders (5) – Staff Burnout. WHO Division of Mental Health No. who/mnh/mnd/94.21. Geneva

Wright S 2005 Reflections on Spirituality and Health. Wiley. Chichester

Wright S 2006 Burnout – a spiritual crisis. RCN Publications. Harrow

Wright S 2009 Coming Home – notes for the journey. SSP. Cumbria

Wright S and Sayre-Adams J 2009 (3rd edition) Sacred Space – right relationship and spirituality in health care. SSP. Cumbria

Zohar D and Marshall I 2000 Spiritual intelligence: the ultimate intelligence. Bloomsbury. London